Max et Mathilde ™

Je m'appelle:

My name is:

....

A few tips for grown-ups!

The book and CD can be used on different levels. The left-hand page introduces the child to a single word. This word is then included in a simple sentence. Stick to this if that's what you feel is most appropriate.

On the right-hand page, the dialogue delivered by Max et Mathilde introduces a slightly higher level of vocabulary and expression.

Let the pictures guide the child. A translation appears at the back of the book rather than on the page itself, to avoid word-for-word translation.

Pronunciation is modelled by Max et Mathilde on the audio CD. Repetition and singing along will reinforce the vocabulary and phrases in the book.

The most important thing is to maintain the child's enthusiasm, motivation and interest in learning French. Above all, keep it simple and fun!

rouge

Les ballons sont rouges.

1 un
2 deux
3 trois
4 quatre
5 cinq

Il y a cinq ballons.

jaune

Les fleurs sont jaunes.

vert

L'arbre est vert.

noir

Le parapluie est noir.

orange

Les carottes sont oranges.

rose

La glace est rose.

bleu

Le ciel est bleu.

Translations and Questions

Page 3

"Bonjour!" *"Hello!"*
Tu vas apprendre tes couleurs. *You're going to learn your colours.*
Tu vas t'amuser! *You'll have fun!*
"Je m'appelle Max." *" My name is Max."*
"Je m'appelle Mathilde." *"My name is Mathilde."*
Le chien s'appelle Noisette. *The dog's name is Noisette.*

4-5

Rouge Red
Les ballons sont rouges. The balloons are red.
"Un, deux, trois, quatre, cinq." *"One, two, three, four, five."*
"Il y a cinq ballons." *"There are five balloons."*
Ask the child how many balloons there are: **"Combien de ballons y-a-t-il?"**

6-7

Jaune Yellow
Les fleurs sont jaunes. The flowers are yellow.
"Regarde-moi!" *"Look at me!"*
Ask the child to find the yellow butterfly: **"Trouve le papillon jaune!"**

8-9

Vert Green
L'arbre est vert. The tree is green.
"Nous jouons dans le jardin." *"We're playing in the garden."*
Ask if the child likes playing in the garden: **"Aimes-tu jouer dans le jardin?"**

Noir Black

Le parapluie est noir. The umbrella is black.

"Il pleut." "It is raining."

"Nous sommes tristes." " We are sad."

Ask what the weather is like: **"Quel temps fait-il?"**

Orange Orange

Les carottes sont oranges. The carrots are orange.

"J'adore manger des carottes!" "I love eating carrots!"

"Moi, je déteste les carottes!" "I hate carrots!"

Ask what colour the carrots are: **"De quelle couleur sont les carottes?"**

Rose Pink.

La glace est rose. The ice cream is pink.

"Je mange une glace à la fraise." "I am eating a strawberry ice cream."

"Je bois de la limonade." "I am drinking lemonade."

Ask if the child likes ice cream: **"Aimes-tu la glace?"**

Bleu Blue

Le ciel est bleu. The sky is blue.

"Regarde le bateau, Max!" "Look at the boat, Max!"

Ask what colour the boat is: **"De quelle couleur est le bateau?"**

Now listen to Max et Mathilde on the CD
as they take you through the colours.
Chant out loud and sing along with them!

Les Couleurs

Rouge et jaune,
Vert et noir,
Toutes les couleurs
.Nous allons voir!
Orange et rose,
Le ciel est bleu.
Regarde avec nous
Les jolies couleurs!

The Colours
Red and yellow, green and black, we're going to see
all the colours! Orange and pink, the sky is blue. Look at the pretty colours with us!

"À bientôt!"